Everything Without Content 242

Verlag der Buchhandlung Walther und Franz König, Köln

Photographs by Stefano Graziani

Itsuko Hasegawa

Shonandai

Exposing the World

Contents

p. 6 Exposing the World

16 Shonandai Cultural Centre

138 Almost Light Architecture

Exposing the World

'In 1968, the year I started graduate studies at the Tokyo Institute of Technology, an article in the Austrian magazine *Bau* about Hans Hollein's revolutionary new thesis that "Everything is Architecture" had a huge impact on me. His words could be taken as a denial of modernism, and I soon felt that architecture included non-material things like air and states of being.'[1]
—Itsuko Hasegawa

Bau: Magazine for Architecture and Urban Planning, issue 1/2, 1968 (photography Stefano Graziani)

A month before the ill-fated opening of the 1968 Milan Triennale, Hans Hollein used his editorship of *Bau* magazine to publish his radical manifesto *Alles ist Architektur*. The phrase, borrowed from Le Corbusier, was an explicit reference to the modernist belief in the totalizing capacity of architecture, but here the notion of 'everything' was expanded ad absurdum. As if copied from a Team 10 workbook, Hollein's manifesto-magazine opened with the claim: 'Today the environment as a whole is the goal of our activities.' Hollein—who up to then had only built a candle shop in Vienna, and fashioned himself more as an artist than an architect—found the perfect opportunity to test the limits of this ambition when he was commissioned by Giancarlo de Carlo to design the Austrian contribution to the Triennale. *Austriennale* would turn out to be a sort of madcap catalogue of environments, a recursive scenography of (Austrian) reality. Visitors were faced with a series of doors: to a refrigerated corridor with artificial snowstorms, to a hall of mirrors, to a room full of filing cabinets, to a corridor with many doors that could not open, marked simply 'frustration'. A machine churned out plastic glasses in the red and white stripes of the Austrian flag that allowed one to 'see things through Austrian eyes'. Architecture was dissolved into the technological production

1 Itsuko Hasegawa, 'My Theory of Architecture', *Japan SPOTLIGHT*, no. 133 (January/February 2004).

of special effects, an immaterial simulation of the world; it could come in aerosol or pill form, or it could be seen through glasses. But no matter how indefinable the message, the Triennale still got ransacked.

Ultimately, architecture-as-environment was a dead-end of the techno-utopian avant-garde. In the aftermath of '68, the unwavering faith in architecture and technological progress to bring about social change seemed conspicuously naïve, all the gadgets and gizmos utterly frivolous. The future didn't come in the shape of pills or sci-fi machines. The information age was ostensibly lacking in form, and its focus was elsewhere in any case, first in America and then in Japan, which had embarked on what looked like a miraculous path—from an obliterated nation, bombed and then occupied by the US, to what threatened to become the world's largest economy. Japan's rate of growth, seemingly unstoppable, accelerated further after the 1973 oil crisis, when it shifted to a new type of booming industry: digital technology and electronic materials, cars and TVs, computers and robotics. The prosperity of the early 1980s fuelled a rapid turnover of property and land—and one of the biggest asset price bubbles of all time. Architecture became a disposable business. Never worth more than the value of the plot, buildings were merely temporary assets, with a typical lifespan of less than ten years. Gone were the days of the Metabolist avant-garde concern for the city and utopian urban systems, as the market favoured the small-scale, the experimental, and the temporary. Like Shinto shrines, continually torn down and rebuilt, this novel real-estate frenzy sought longevity through constant renewal. Sturdy postwar concrete architecture gave way to something more ephemeral, of little material substance, embracing the protean urbanity. The new industrial vernacular enacted an aesthetic of transience as a hyper-modern condition of the megalopolis, where architecture is nothing more than a minimal definition of shelter for urban nomads.

In 1986, the same year the economic bubble began to inflate, an open competition was held for a cultural centre in Shonandai, a newly developed area in the north of Fujisawa, one of the many commuter towns for Tokyo and Yokohama. The jury, which notably included Arata Isozaki and Fumihiko Maki, chose the project by Itsuko Hasegawa, who at the time had built only a handful of private houses and had never taken part in a competition before. Hasegawa's winning project, together with the eerily similar entries of her counterparts Toyo Ito and Kazunari Sakamoto, was representative of a new aesthetic that contemporary critics began to call 'light' architecture.

Shonandai was built from scratch in the 1960s around the Shonandai train station, from which it got its name. With a population of 20,000, it was part of a larger land redevelopment project to provide housing and commuting for the workers of companies like Isuzu Motors. The cultural centre was a sort of hybrid typology to bring about the non-existent city, combining a public theatre, a civic centre with offices and sport facilities, and a children's museum with a planetarium. The designated site was an 8,000 sqm vacant lot, once hilly agricultural terrain, now razed for the new town development—a desolate land in a rural area, with cabbage fields next to new apartment buildings. Taking 'architecture as landscape' as her pretext (and project title), Hasegawa proposed the ultimate disappearing act of architecture, effectively burying the whole thing underground. When the perplexed town officials later asked Hasegawa why she wanted to bury the building, she explained: 'We're not building a building. We're rebuilding the field that was there before.' In a context where everything was disposable and quickly produced, even nature could be manmade. This nostalgic re-enactment took on a prodigious form. There was the Universe—a large sunken sphere that enclosed an 800-seat theatre, clad in aluminium to reflect the sky. The globe-like smaller sphere of the planetarium represented the Earth. A third sphere was the Moon. There was also a geodesic dome, and a heliometer, and an open-air theatre, and a tiled stream, and a Chinese garden, and a Japanese bridge over an artificial pond, complete with swans. Clusters of triangular skylights emulated a forest, while the entire undulating surface of the complex was reminiscent of the razed hills, now (re)constructed as a gigantic accumulation of building material. There were vine-hung stainless-steel pergolas, perforated-metal trees, and a myriad of other things—some ultimately unrealised, like the entrance in the shape of a pyramid. If the idea was, as Hasegawa would have it, to keep the vacant site vacant, the end result was a scene of sheer abundance.

In reality, for the building to disappear, the trick was not so much to bury it, as to hide it in plain sight. As long as the status of the building was mitigated to that of an environment, there was no hierarchy, no differences, and thus no sense of monumentality. The artificial nature became an exercise in white noise, an act of hyper-densification creating some sort of vacuum of meaning. A plethora of *things* became an elaborate subterfuge to avoid making architecture. Instead, Hasegawa was on a mission to *describe* the environment by inventorying everything in it.

Her idea of expressing nature and the universe in high-tech detailing—what she called the 'architecturalisation of nature'—was meant to imply a flexible outlook on the contemporary world. The world is whatever we make of it, as *there is no classification of the universe that is not arbitrary and full of conjectures.* The project, in other words, is a matter of selecting, rather than designing. Architecture can look like anything it is supposed to symbolise. What is unique about the complex, however, is that each element in it stubbornly maintains its own identity: it doesn't refer to something other than itself but is simply what it is, in its own dodged, somewhat mutated way. Hasegawa seemed to think only the awkwardness of the literal presence of an element would free the citizen from an a-priori use. Since everything is simplified, and nothing really used in the way the origin of it would suggest, each feature of this enormous complex hints at radical liberation—liberation from function, but ultimately also from form. When *everything is architecture*, somehow nothing really remains architecture; rather, it suddenly becomes a pending natural condition, as some sort of constructed backdrop for things to happen: a second nature.

In the absence of a real distinction between the natural and the artificial environment, there is no real threshold between inside and outside, and no difference between architecture and decoration. Trees, clouds, planets, hills, forests are all some sort of abstracted version of the real thing, as a gigantic decor piece made out of metal and concrete. The heart of the complex is—unsurprisingly—the children's museum, a place that in any other context would be an exercise in interior decoration. Hasegawa, however, understood this particular creation of *a world within the world* as the possible origin of the whole Shonandai complex. For the museum she designed insects and dinosaur eggs and planets ... objects are scaled up or down to make them more tangible (for children) and their casual distribution organises the space. Space is thus a mere consequence—and not the prerequisite—of the presence of objects and shapes. The figures make the space (of the artificial Shonandai hill) usable: their composition, precise as it is, suggests a certain randomness, a looseness that manages to expose the world as it is. This deceptive looseness is the driving force of the design process at play. Any figure can be activated in this game of casual conversation. The planetarium is a globe, but the theatre is a globe too, albeit one that uses the qualities of the sphere to defy theatrical conventions. Rooftops of forest-like huts serve as lightwells and for ventilation. A tree could also be a lamppost. Glass marbles form a star-studded ceiling in the planetarium, and re-appear in the custom-made chairs all over the complex. Subtly, the conventions of the thing and the representation of the thing are transgressed in favour of a wilder idea of architecture where everything is allowed to exist as long as it shows some inner coherence—enough coherence, at least, to be put under pressure by weird additions or modifications. The architecture of the project assimilates the motley objects and activities, unwittingly fostering its populist appeal.

It is precisely this combination of spaced-out imagery and pragmatic know-how that gives the Shonandai cultural centre an air of unpretentious realism. Even if the imagery is decidedly eccentric, the execution is not: craziness got a down-to-earth translation, combining industrial and traditional, often handmade materials. Participation and improvisation were not some kind of ideological posturing, but a common-sense practice, even a necessity. The building was completed in 1990, the same year that Japan's fabled economic bubble abruptly burst. Local craftsmen, citizens and even students had to be drafted in to minimise costs. There was no money for the aluminium cladding of the dome, so thermal spray aluminium was used instead. Anything could be adapted, anybody could contribute or have an opinion, forging civic participation as an aspect of the collective use of the building. This liberal openness and radical saturation made an escape from monumental and functionalist modernism possible. The tropes and figures that Hasegawa uses are decidedly modern, but also overabundant and out of scale. Despite all the perforated aluminium screens, her version of "light" architecture is still heavy with meaning and full of things—the building is not only stimulating events, but is an event in itself. Relentlessly rearranging and accumulating these 'scenes' in a bountiful collection and stacking them together until the totality of it is about to explode is a way of making *light* through *heavy*, as some sort of ultimate act of densification before its eventual release. Itsuko Hasegawa's Shonandai cultural centre exploded the modern project, once and —until now in Japan at least—for all. Anything after that became quasi-invisible.

Itsuko Hasegawa (1941) studied in the Department of Architecture at Kanto Gakuin University in Yokohama. Upon graduating in 1964, she worked for Kiyonori Kikutake, where she was joined by Toyo Ito a year later. She left Kikutake's office to enrol in the lab of Kazuo Shinohara at the Tokyo Institute of Technology, first as a student, and then as his assistant and only full-time office employee. In parallel, Hasegawa pursued her own projects, building six houses and one commercial building while working for Shinohara. She set up her own practice in 1979 after receiving her first big commission (for the Tokumaru children's clinic). She would realise several houses, commercial buildings and a high-school dormitory (Bizan Hall) before entering an open architectural competition for the first time in late 1985. The following year, it was announced that Hasegawa had won the first prize: the Shonandai cultural centre, her first public building, would be completed in 1990.

CLUB
S
NAS KIDS
NAS
P
湘南台文化センター
利用者専用駐車場
止まれ
三井眼科

放置禁止

この道路は駐車禁止です
正しいルールとマナーを守りましょう
藤沢警察署
藤沢市

-2

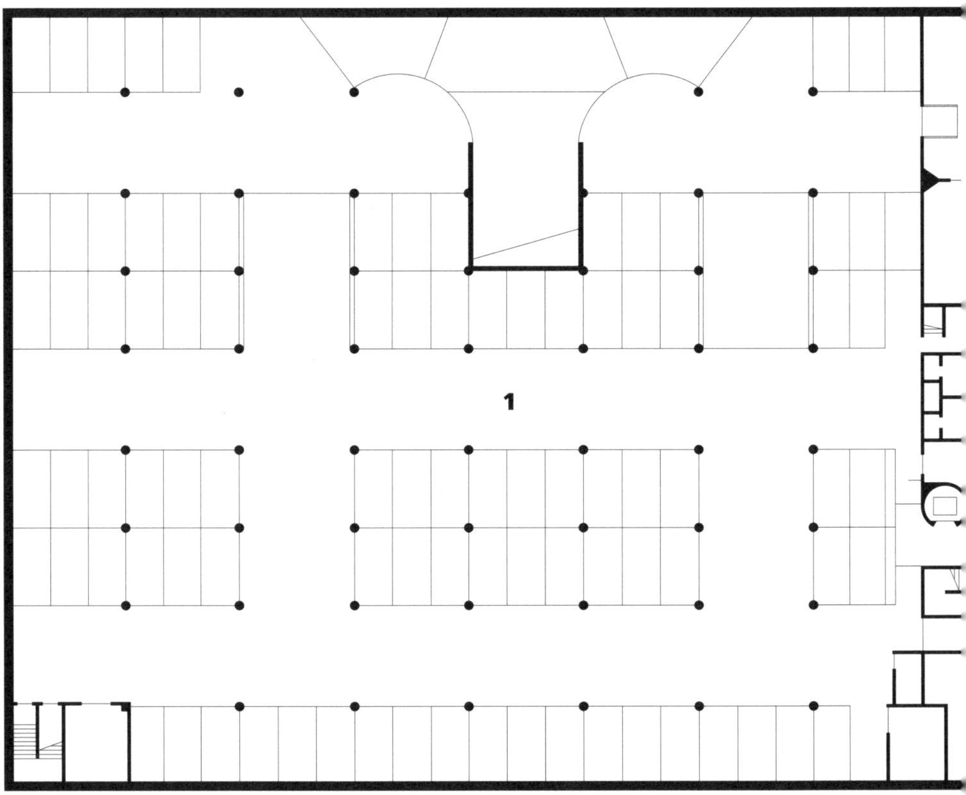

1 / 500

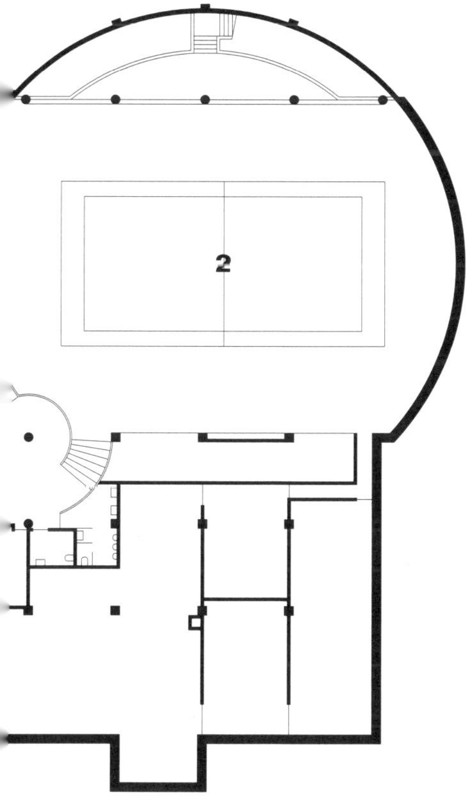

1 **Parking**
2 **Gymnasium**

空車
駅地下
P

田中土建工業

50

ご注意

+0

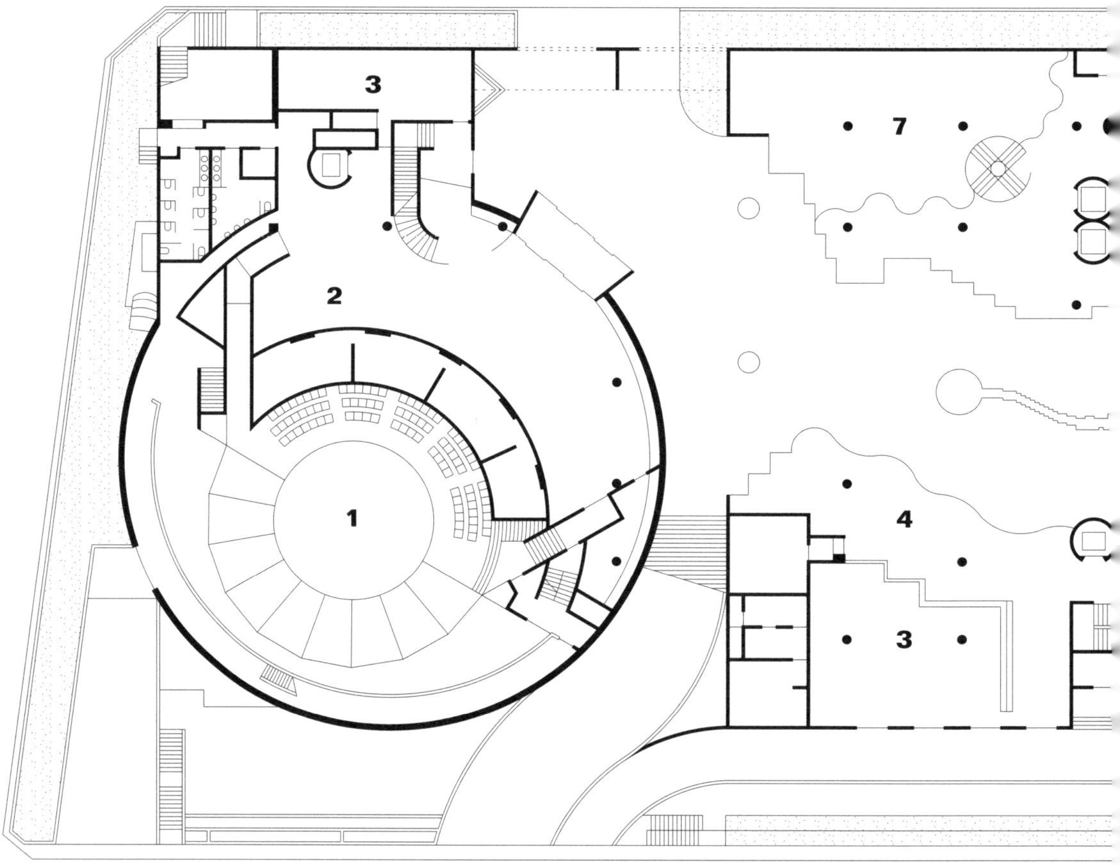

1 / 500

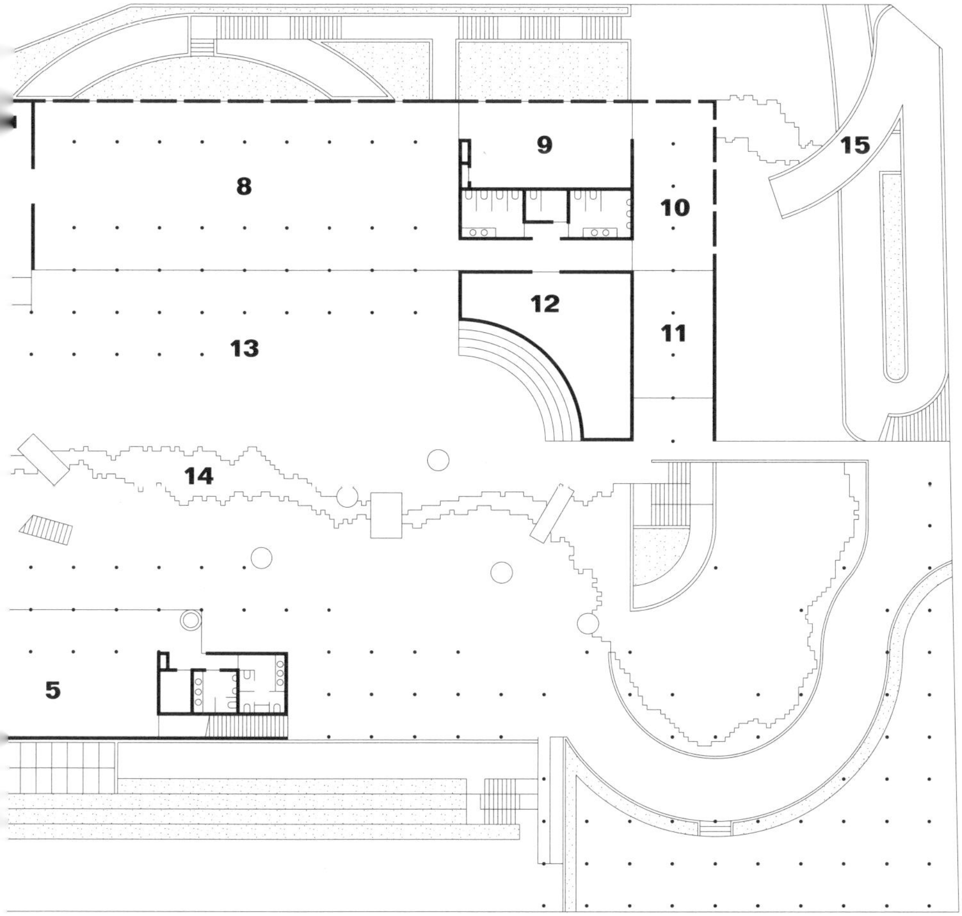

1 Theatre stage
2 Lobby
3 Office
4 Civic centre hall
5 Gallery
6 Children's museum hall
7 Void
8 Children's museum workshop
9 Laboratory
10 Terrace
11 Pottery room
12 Storage
13 Plaza
14 Stream
15 Ramp access

田中土建工業

田中土建工業

市民シアター
会場予約

市民シアター
Civic Theatre
大変滑りやすくなっております。足元には十分注意して御通行下さい。
市民シアター
会場予約

市民シアター
au

市民シアター
Civic Theatre
市民シアター
Civic Theatre
こども館

じてんしゃ
はいれません

民シアター
Civic Theatre

防犯カメラ作動中
市民シアター

+1

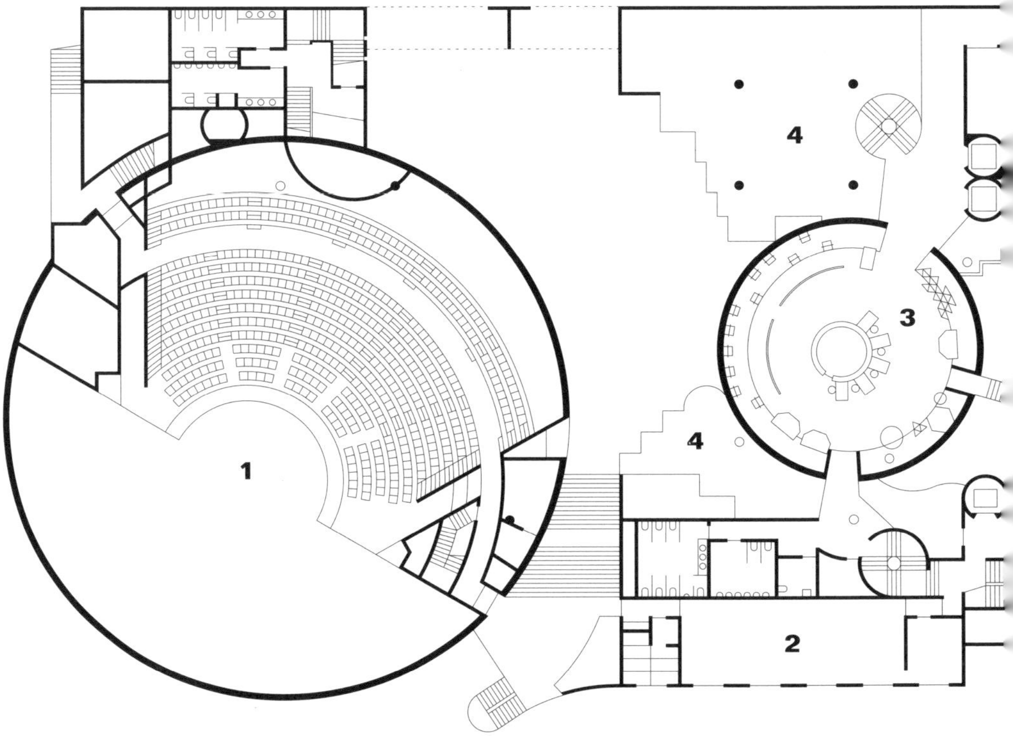

1 / 500

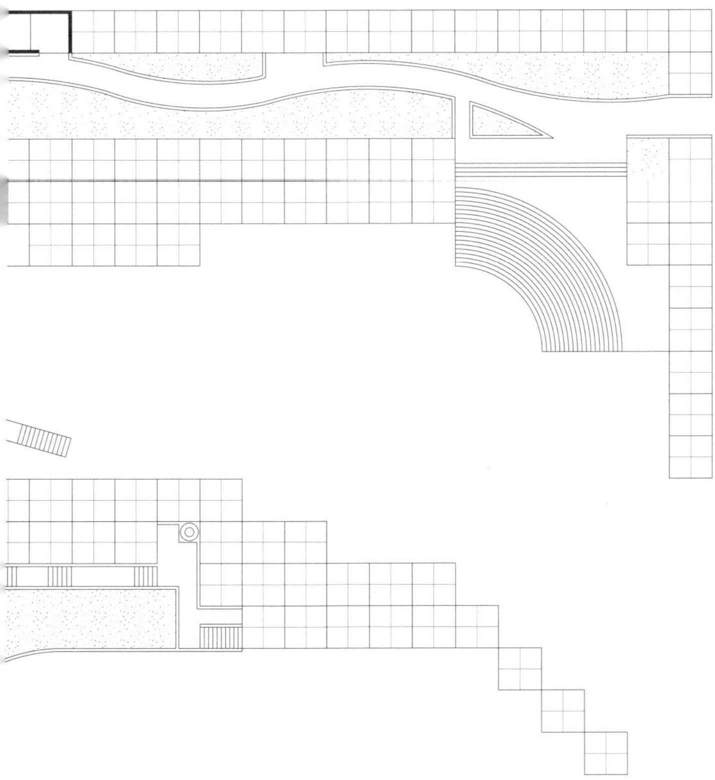

1 **Theatre stage**
2 **Office**
3 **Planetarium gallery**
4 **Void**

こども館
プラネ
タリウム
ワーク
ショップ
入口
はこちら

こども館
プラネ タリウム
ワーク ショップ
入口
はこちら
Asahi
SOFT DRINKS

藤沢市からのお知らせ
藤沢市からのお知らせ
湘南台地区
定期刊行物

←④公民館
地域団体
←受付
ちょこっとしょかん
どなたでもご利用できます。
公民館利用者 専用認証機
湘南台小学校 運営委員会
ご協力よろしくお願いします。

浮世絵とみる
昔の暮らしの道具
7.13
9.8
足元注意願います。

← ④ 公民館
地域団体
← 受付
ちょこっと
としょかん
湘南台小学校
運営委員会
ご協力よろしくお願いします。
雨漏り、
足元注意願います。
湘南台文化センター

-1

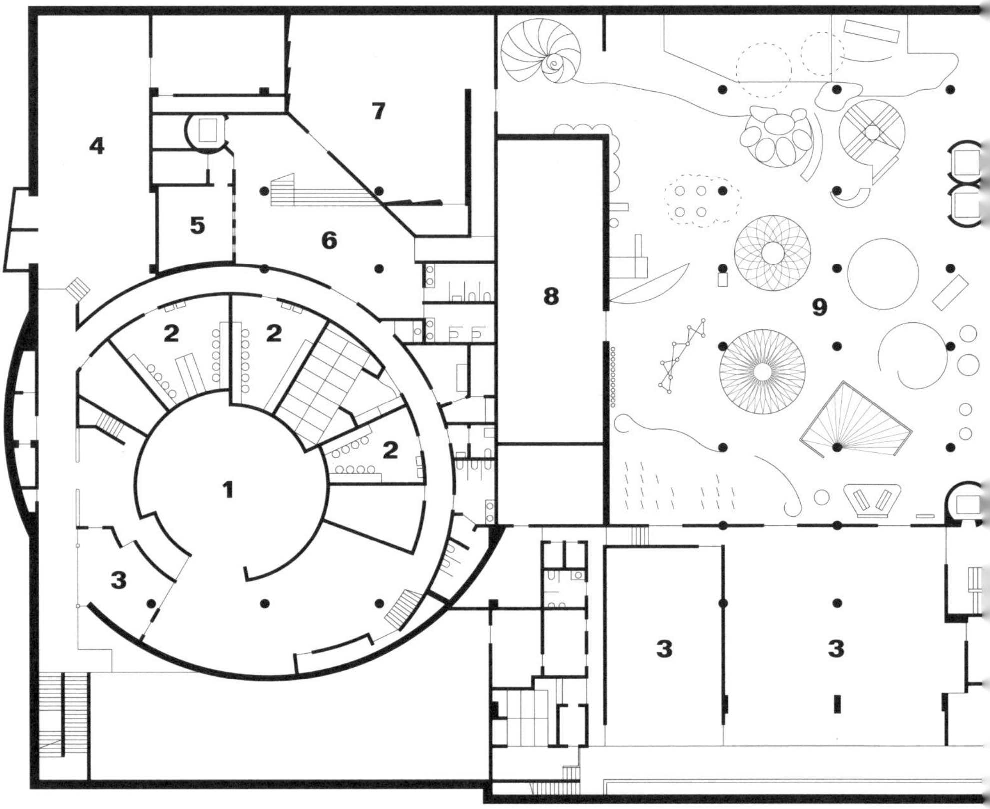

1 / 500

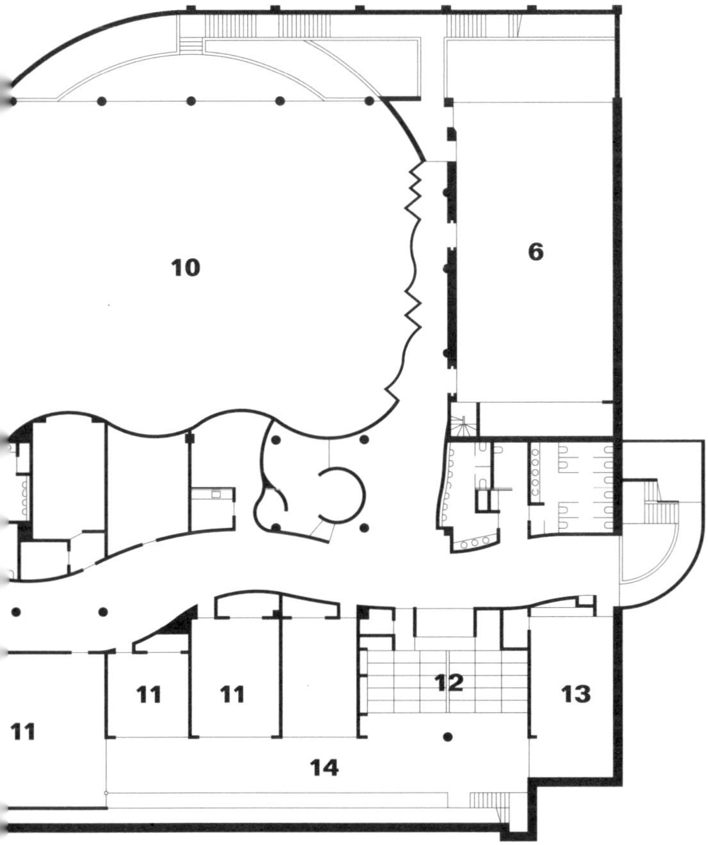

1 Theatre stage (trap room)
2 Dressing rooms
3 Office
4 Mechanical room
5 Studio
6 Lobby
7 Rehearsal room
8 Parking ramp
9 Children's museum exhibition hall
10 Void
11 Lounge
12 Tatami room
13 Kitchen
14 Sunken garden

会場予約
飲食は、こちらのスペースで
お願いします。
ゴミは、お持ち帰りください。
荷物置き場は、各階の荷物棚を
ご利用ください。
食べこぼしなど、汚れた場合は、
各自お片付けください。
ご利用は 17:00 までお願いします

MISSION! スタンプラリー
スタンプ
ラリー
月面着陸は
どこ！？
の着陸地点を月バルーンで想像してみよう！
何の模様？？
3
2
1
B1

スペースで
ます。
ち帰りください。
は、各階の荷物棚を
さい。
しなど、汚れた場合は、
付けください。
までお願いします

どこの国かな？
クイズ①
ヒント

ちえのわ
コーナー

カーブした鏡

+2

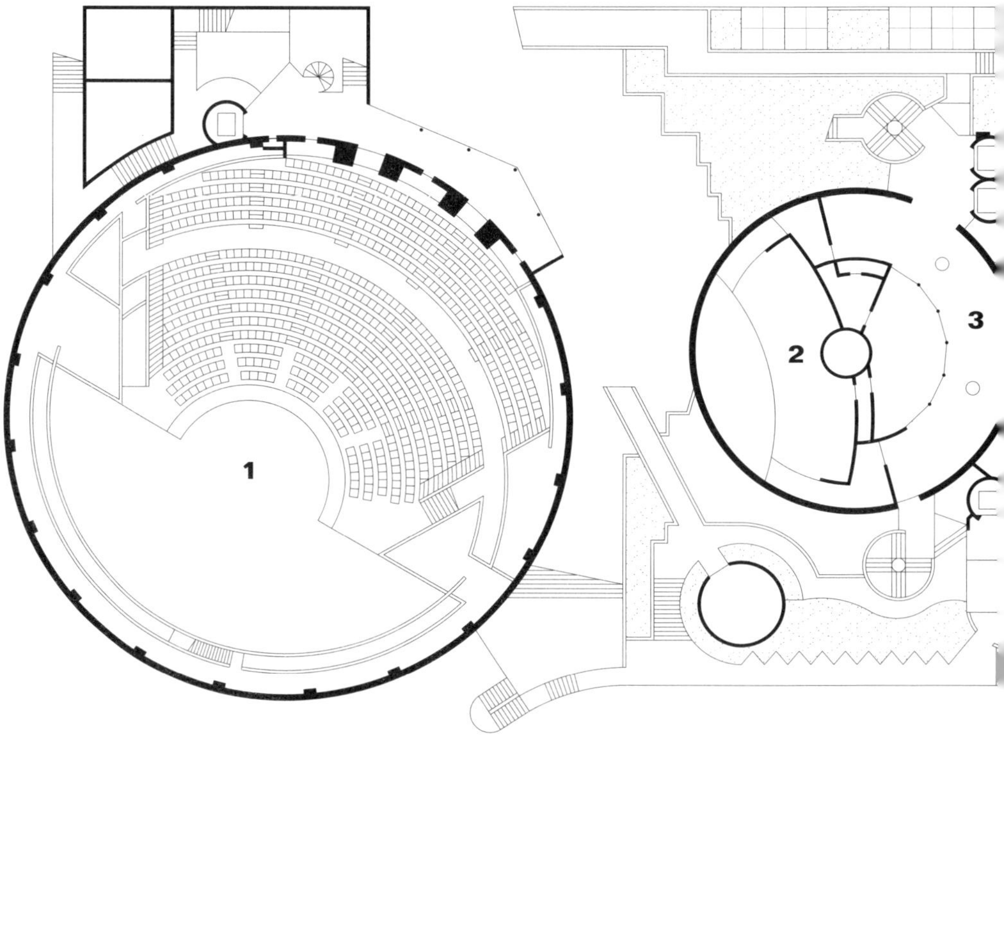

1 / 500

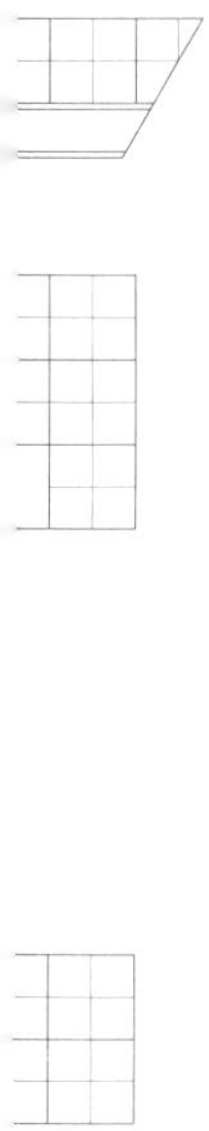

1 Theatre
2 Planetarium
3 Lobby
4 Radio room

トイレ
「はやぶさ2」
できたよ！
見つけたよ！

HII-A ロケット
第2段 液体水素タンク
第2段エンジン
第1段 主エンジン
第2段 液体酸素タンク
第1段 液体酸素タンク
固体ロケットブースター

アースラボ
太陽系の惑星たち
OUR SOLAR SYSTEM
はいらない
木星
土星

惑星の重さ比べ
金星
地球
火星
土星
天王星
海王星
ここでは飲まないでネ！
2階で
飲み物を飲むときは
パソコンのお部屋の
外でお願いします
消火器

近赤外線
近紫外線
遠紫外線
軟X線
硬X線
外線
紫外線
エックス線
ガンマ線
●波長
●周波数
と、見え方が変わります
紫外線
エックス(X)線
可視光線
ナニガミエル?
ドコカラミル?
見え方のちがい
2000万光年離れたところにある、おおぐま座の回転花火銀河(M101)を、
いろいろな波長で見てみましょう。

お手洗

6
5
4
ゆかいなくるま大集合！
華麗な蝶たちの世界

3
こどもにんぎょう劇場
1. 赤ずきん
2. 最後の一葉
3. ぎざみみうさぎ
立方体
正4面体
多面体 120枚
正12面体
諏訪間 和広
青木 優介

+3

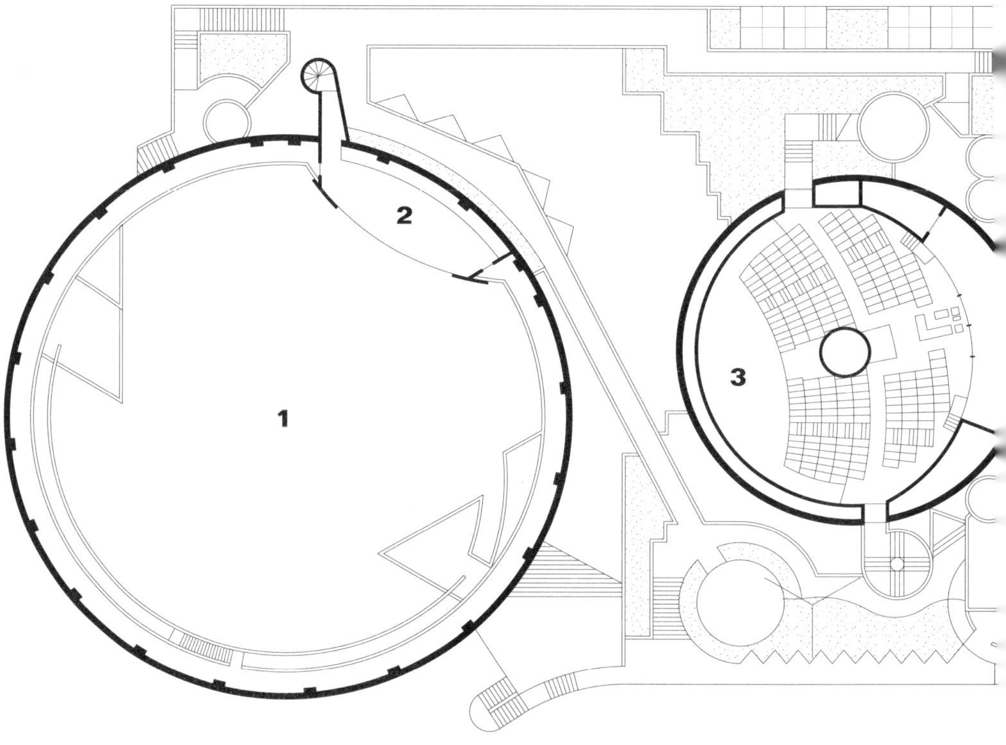

1 / 500

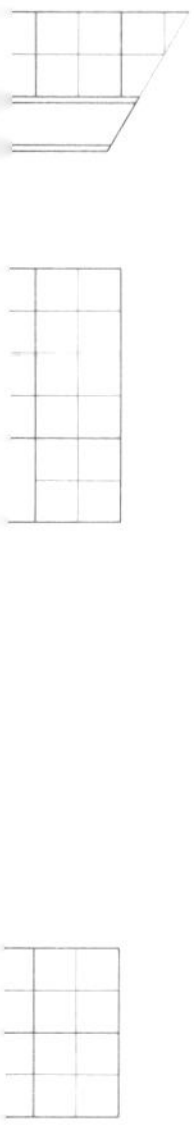

1 Theatre
2 Control room
3 Planetarium

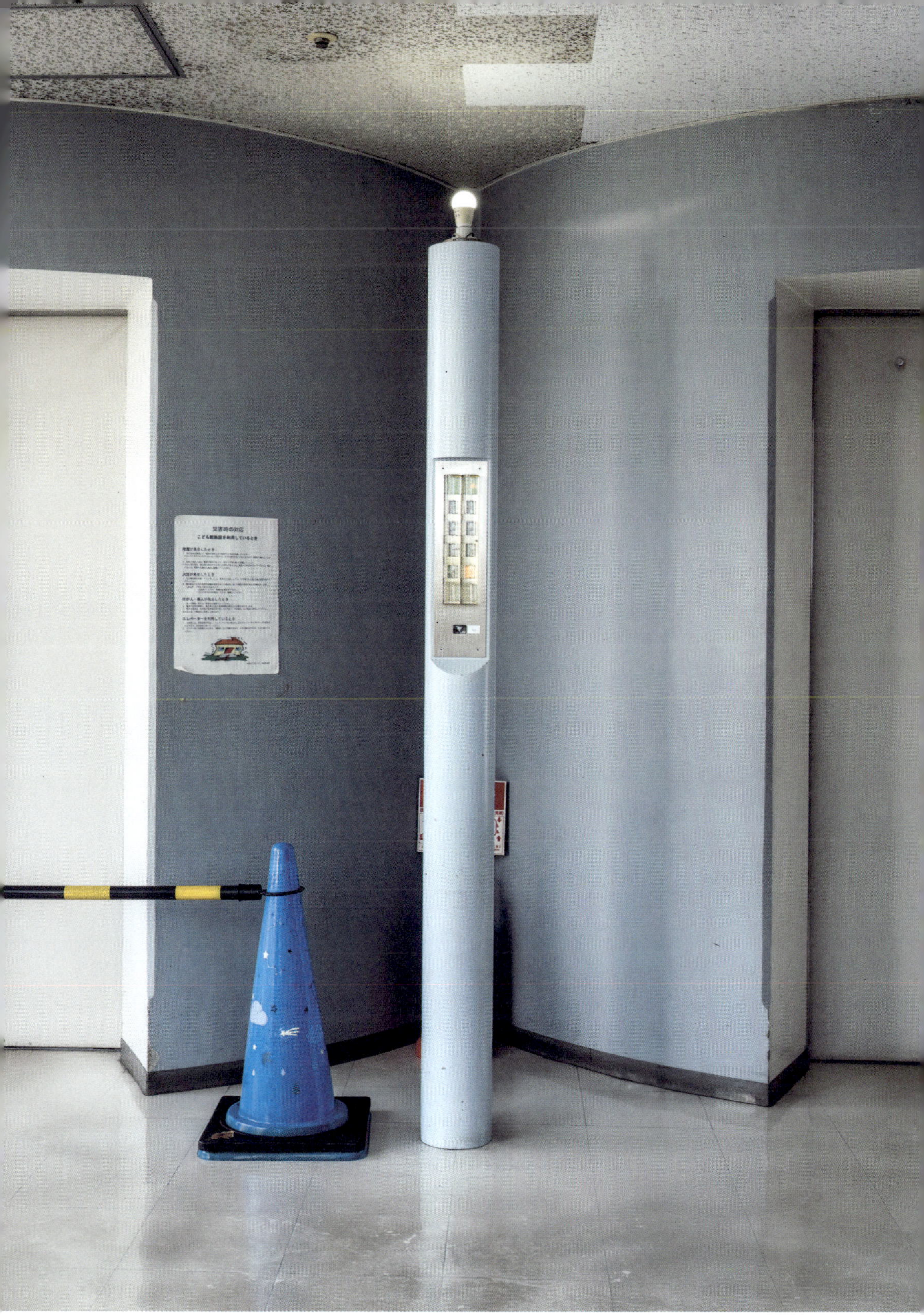
災害時の対応

入口
出口

入口

内科

出られません
ここから外に
ないでください

NAS KIDS
湘南台文化センター
利用者専用駐輪場
止まれ
三井眼科

Roof plan

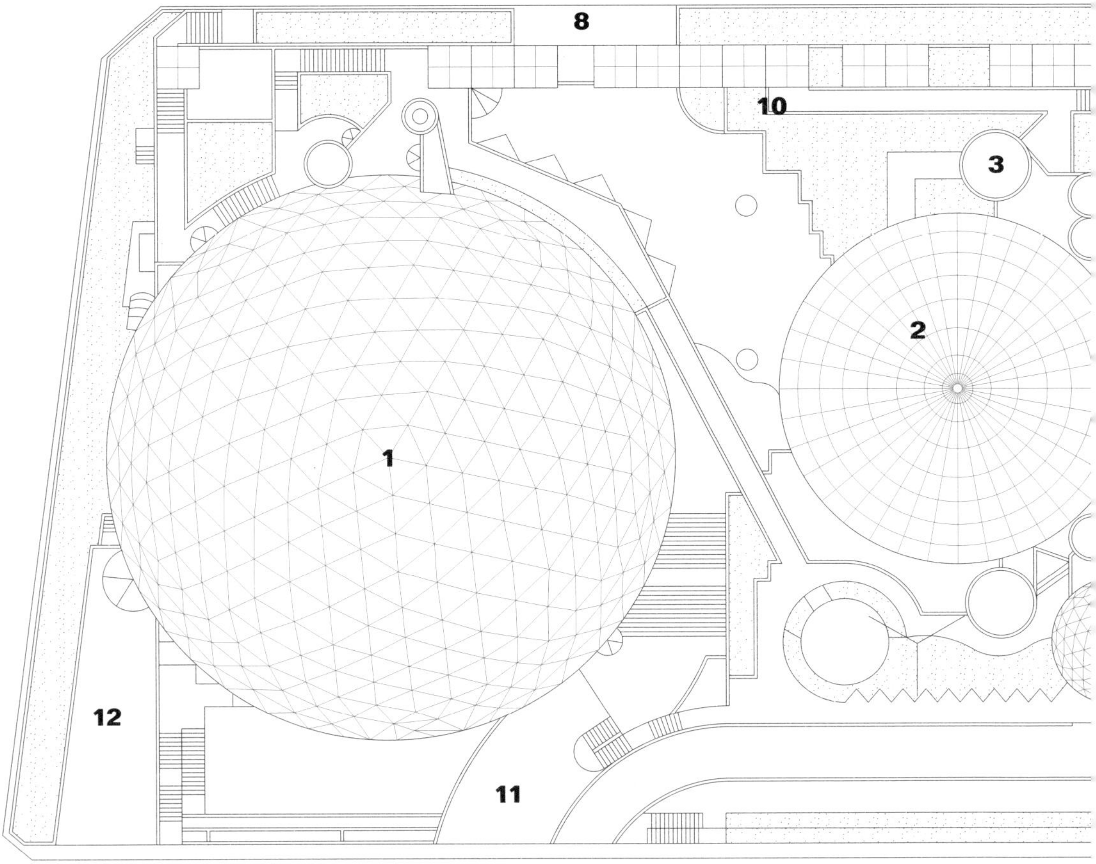

1 / 500

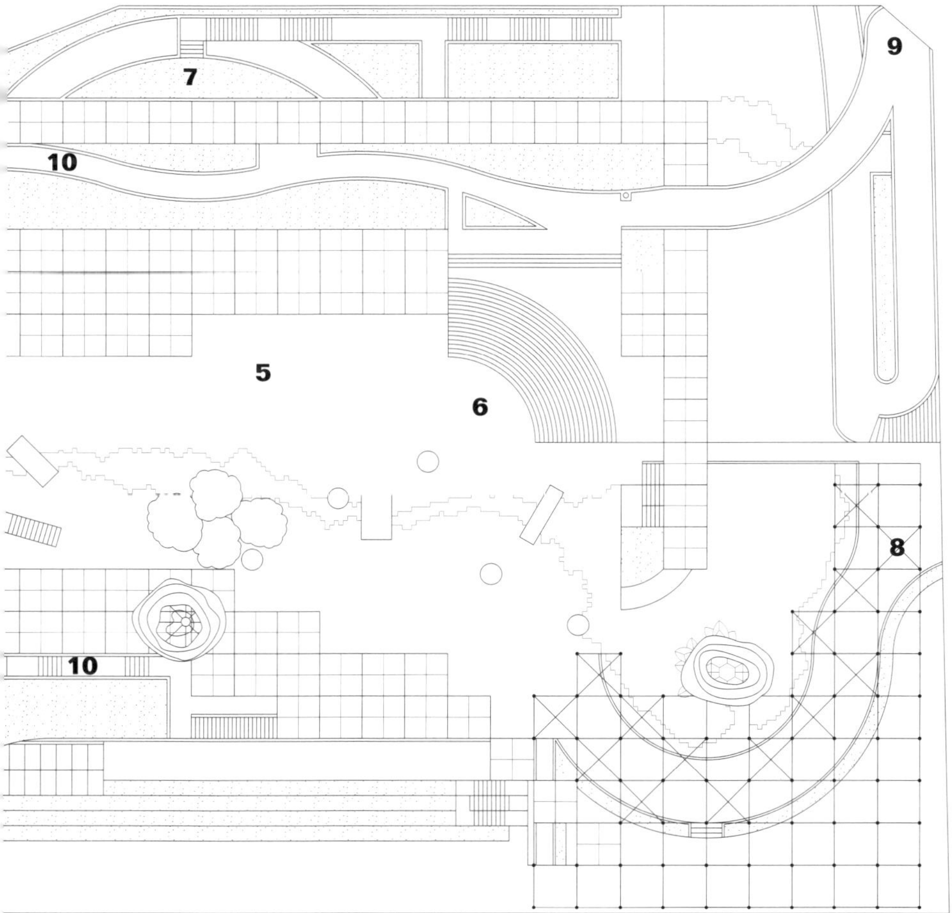

1 Theatre
2 Planetarium
3 Heliometer
4 Geodesic dome
5 Plaza
6 Open-air theatre
7 Garden
8 Entrance
9 Bridge to the Shonandai park
10 Walkway
11 Parking entrance
12 Backstage entrance

Section

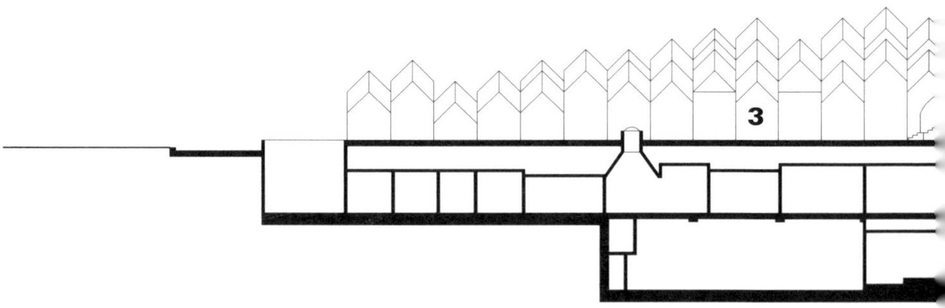

1 / 500

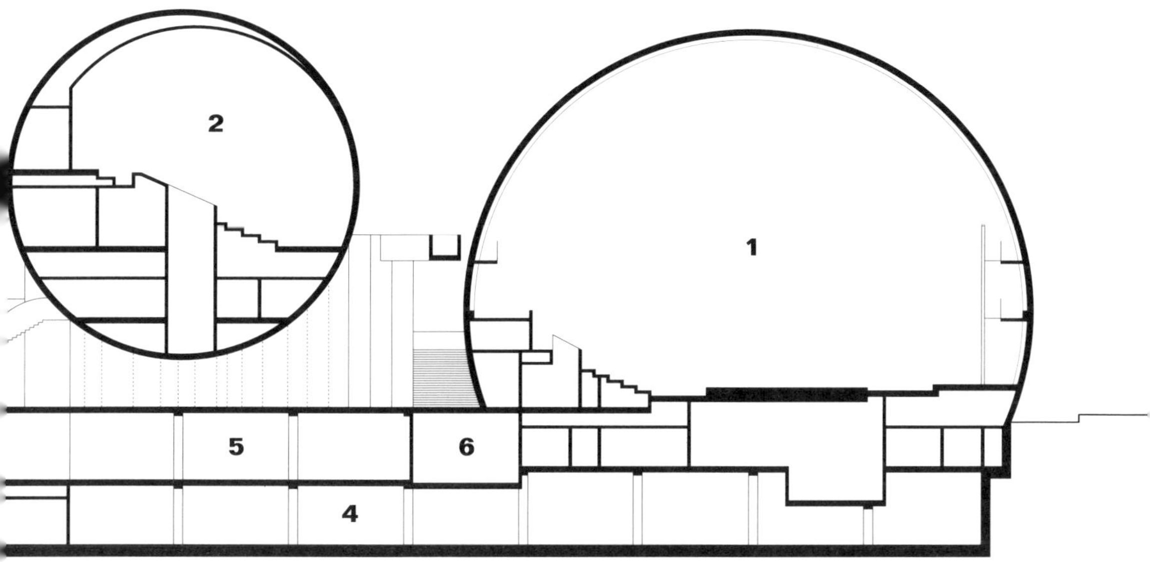

1 **Theatre**
2 **Planetarium**
3 **Plaza**
4 **Parking**
5 **Children's museum**
6 **Parking ramp**

South elevation 1 / 500

North elevation 1 / 500

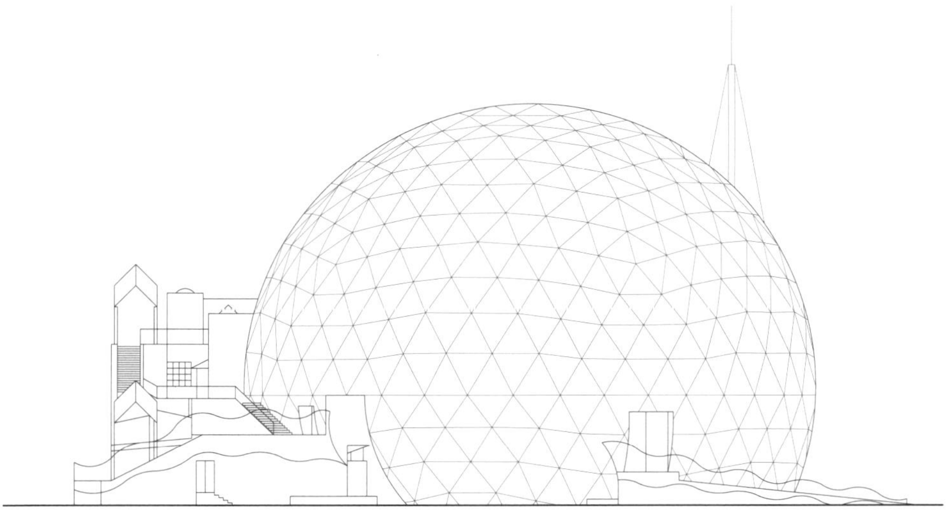

East elevation

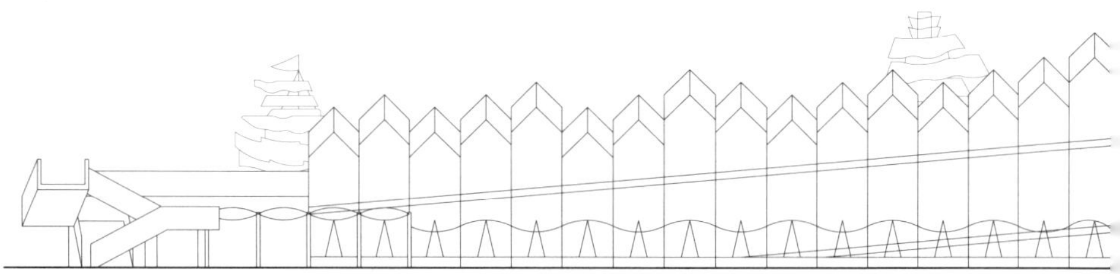

1 / 500

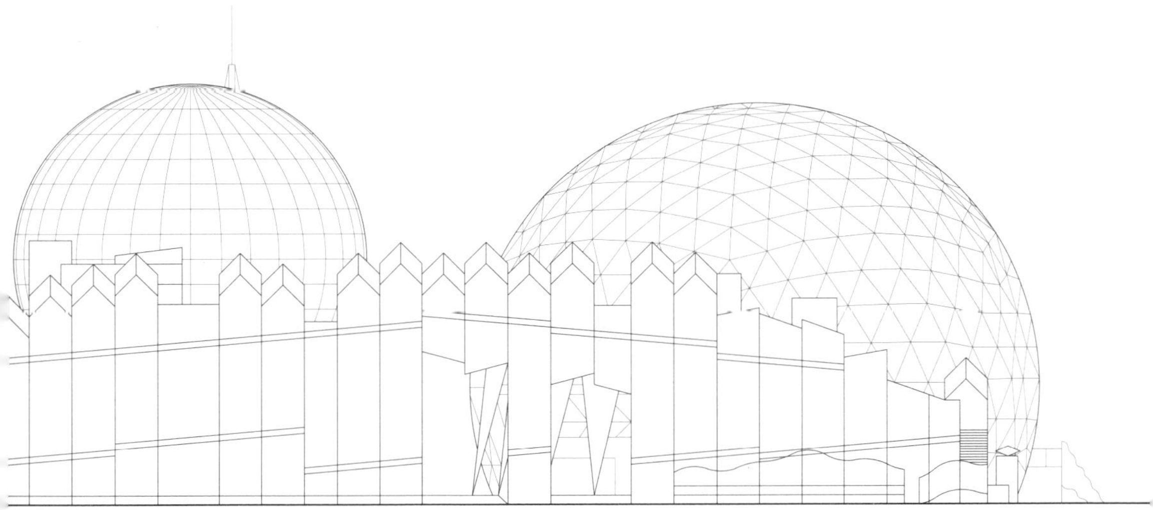

West elevation

1 / 500

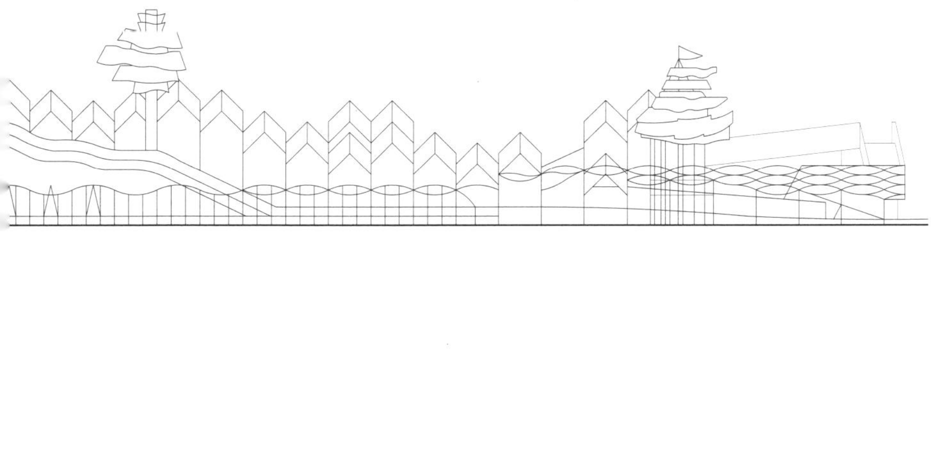

Almost Light Architecture

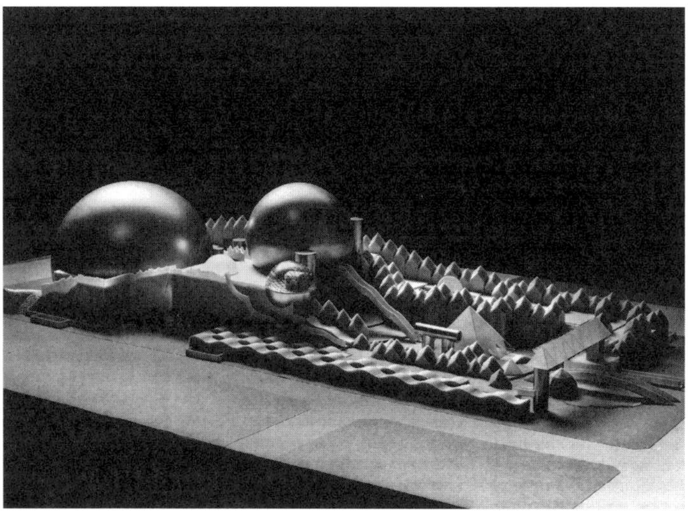

Itsuko Hasegawa, competition model for the Shonandai Cultural Centre (1986)

Of the two hundred and fifteen entries submitted to the Shonandai cultural centre competition in 1986, three stood out. Itsuko Hasegawa, Toyo Ito and Kazunari Sakamoto all proposed versions of landscape-like buildings that broke with the modernist credo of monumental and authoritative public architecture. The cohort, known as the 'Shinohara school', had similar origin stories. Like the master himself, they too had embraced the freedom from urban design and had made small, experimental houses as private utopias. Theirs was an ambivalent alliance, each having their own complex and often difficult relationship with Kazuo Shinohara. Ito was a fan; Sakamoto his student and assistant; Hasegawa his student, assistant and, before she opened her own practice in 1979, his only full-time employee. What they all shared was the conviction that the profound weightlessness of the Japanese consumer society called for a fresh and partly disposable formal language; a syntax able to translate and deal with the perpetual *newness*. They also shared a penchant for modern industrial materials—expanded meshes, perforated aluminium sheeting and permeable fabrics. They had a common collaborator in the architect-turned-furniture designer Teruaki Ohashi (another Shinohara disciple), whose odd and graphical furniture populated their otherwise bare interiors

Kazunari Sakamoto, competition model for the Shonandai Cultural Centre (1986)

and made possible any idea for living in contemporary Tokyo. These experiments in living developed from some sort of radical formalism—heavy and brutal at first, then geometrical and composed—into complex studies in accumulation and lightness. Hasegawa, Ito and Sakamoto first made houses that exploded and simplified the spatial sequence *inside* and then gradually omitted the roof and the perimeter in the conventional sense, resulting in complex compositions of both form and object, not seldom tent-like.

From this perspective, it is perhaps not surprising that their entries for Shonandai were eerily alike. All three projects independently proposed a building as an artificial landscape, populated by light structures. Each came up with at least two domes and an array of lightweight roofs. They all pointed out the difference between the sunken interior and the floating, village-like public space above—transient and disordered—where somehow anything could happen. In Sakamoto's rendition, the complex was covered by a metallic geodesic roof that turned the building into a kind of suspended megastructure. Ito was even more explicit in his embrace of the temporary, making the whole structure 'collapsible like tents at the bazaar'. Both proposals have features that are remarkably similar to Hasegawa's winning design, stemming from the same preoccupations.

Toyo Ito, competition model for the Shonandai Cultural Centre (1986)

Her project, however, does not share their fatalist approach. Hasegawa's architecture is disabused of metaphors, even if it feeds on them. Landscape is a building; the globe is a building —they are real objects and experiences. Architecture is not temporary, it just makes temporary events possible. All three projects seem to suggest that architecture can somehow *expose the world* and reveal the true nature of the modern, alienating urban condition. But whereas the others resort to an abstract, if not outright apocalyptic imagery, Hasegawa is way more evocative of the immediate environment, and nature. Ito likened his project to a lunar module on the surface of the moon and the theatre to an impact crater, designed with an earth floor and a glass dome. Behind the superficiality of symbols, for him there is only void, literally so. Hasegawa, on the other hand, forges familiar images, and makes architecture as a parallel reality. The chosen imagery made the Shonandai project into some sort of relatable *dream machine*, able to transmute the nomadic and the immaterial into a tangible—but fictional—universe. This was, and still is, the biggest asset and the biggest liability of the project. It takes a light kind of architecture to truly expose the world.

Colophon

Itsuko Hasegawa
Exposing the World

Everything Without
Content 242

Edited by
Kersten Geers,
Jelena Pančevac
Photographs
Stefano Graziani
Texts
Kersten Geers,
Jelena Pančevac
Copy editing
Pamela Johnston
Graphic design
Joris Kritis
Drawings
Marie Bemelmans
Lithography
Elisa Maenhout
Printing
Albe De Coker
Edition
1500 copies

Thanks to
Itsuko Hasegawa
Chie Rokutanda
Seng Kuan
Yoshiharu Tsukamoto
Go Hasegawa
David Van Severen
Margherita Graziani

Publisher
Verlag der
Buchhandlung Walther
und Franz König
Ehrenstr. 4
D–50672 Köln

Distribution
Germany, Austria and
Switzerland
Buchhandlung
Walther König
Ehrenstr. 4,
D–50672 Köln
T+49 (0)2212059653
verlag@buchhandlung-walther-koenig.de

Unites States and
Canada
D.A.P. / Distributed
Art Publishers, Inc.
75 Broad Street,
Suite 630
USA—New York,
NY 10004
T+1 (0)2126271999
orders@dapinc.com

Outside the United
States and Canada,
Germany, Austria and
Switzerland by
Thames & Hudson Ltd.,
London
thamesandhudson.com

ISBN 978-3-7533-0784-8
Printed in Belgium

Bibliographic information
published by the Deutsche
Nationalbibliothek. The
Deutsche Nationalbibliothek lists this publication
in the Deutsche Nationalbibliografie; detailed
bibliographic data are
available on the Internet
at http://dnb.d-nb.de.

Office Without Office
Kersten Geers
David Van Severen